AF479944

Spartanblack©

spartanblack60@gmail.com

Learning how to read easily and well is major hurdle every child must surmount. Mastering the letters of English alphabet is the first step towards reading.

Since alphabets are pronounced differently from how they sound, it is important that children learn the sounds of each alphabet to be able to pronounce English words properly. This is where "Letters made Easy" comes in.

In this book (VOL. 1),children would perfect their mastery of reading the English Language. They would be able to identify key sounds, starting from short vowel sounds, to long vowel sounds and special two letter consonant sounds. All 42 jolly phonics sounds and more have been fully catered for in the series 1-3. Stories that teach them how to pronounce these sounds and strenghten their cognitive abilities are also included, with lots of simple-to-understand new vocabulary. Also, the periodic fact finding exercises are simply irresistible.

This comprehensive book is a must-have for all. Using it either at home or school, children would find great fun in learning how to read! This is an aid to reading not a replacement for learners textbook.

Table of Contents

Table of Contents

a. A B C D E F G H I J K
L M N O P Q R S T U V
W X Y Z

b. Write out the lower case alphabets
   (small letters) from a - z

a b c d e f g h i j k l m
n o p q r s t u v w x y z

c. Write from Aa - Zz

Aa Bb Cc Dd Ee Ff Gg
Hh Ii Jj Kk Ll Mm Nn
Oo Pp Qq Rr Ss Tt Uu
Vv Ww Xx Yy Zz

___ ___ ___ ___ ___ ___ ___

___ ___ ___ ___ ___ ___ ___

___ ___ ___ ___ ___

d. Say each letter and the sound it makes
   from A.....a to Z......z

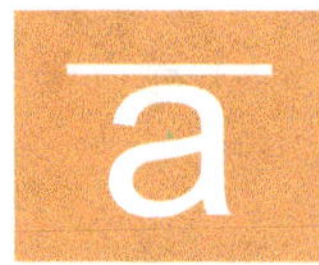

/æ/, /ə/

a. Read these words:

sat	flag	jam	drag
mat	spat	had	tap
nap	trap	clap	hand

Underline the 'a' sound in the words above
b. Some words have the 'a' sound at the begining:

apple	apricot	amp	ask
ankle	ample	adjust	ass
ask	alike	aside	asleep

Underline the 'a' sound
Note: Read each word out to your learners first

c. Some have the 'ā' sound at their end

papa	stamina	alfa
data	pupa	lama
maria	flora	area
jota	gaga	pasta

Underline the ā sound

d. Complete the following words using the 'a' sound

wr_p	st_mp	_mple	gl_d
_rrange	bab_	_nimal	cr_p
pizz_	lam_		

Write five 'a' words for each of these groups:

in the middle	at the begining	at the end
___________	___________	___________
___________	___________	___________
___________	___________	___________
___________	___________	___________
___________	___________	___________

cat   apple   rabbit   mamba
basket   fan   classroom
clap   after   pizza

Using your dictionary, find out the meaning of each word, then make a sentence with each.

cat _____ I have a pet cat. _________________

apple _________________________________

rabbit ________________________________

mamba ________________________________

basket ________________________________

fan ___________________________________

classroom ____________________________

clap __________________________________

after _______________________

____

pizza _______________________

____

Draw a mamba

____

Note:
Help your learners to find out the correct meaning of each word. Have practice sentence making with them first before asking them to make and write theirs.

 /e/

a. Say these words out, then write them out on the lines provided.

pen _____________   web _____________

yet _____________   keg _____________

well _____________   smell _____________

trek _____________   wed _____________

belt _____________   vet _____________

desk _____________   pepper _____________

vest _____________   jester _____________

b. Make your own words up...

get _____________

____

____

____

____

____

____

____

c. Some words have 'e' sound at the beginning.
   Say the words and write them out:

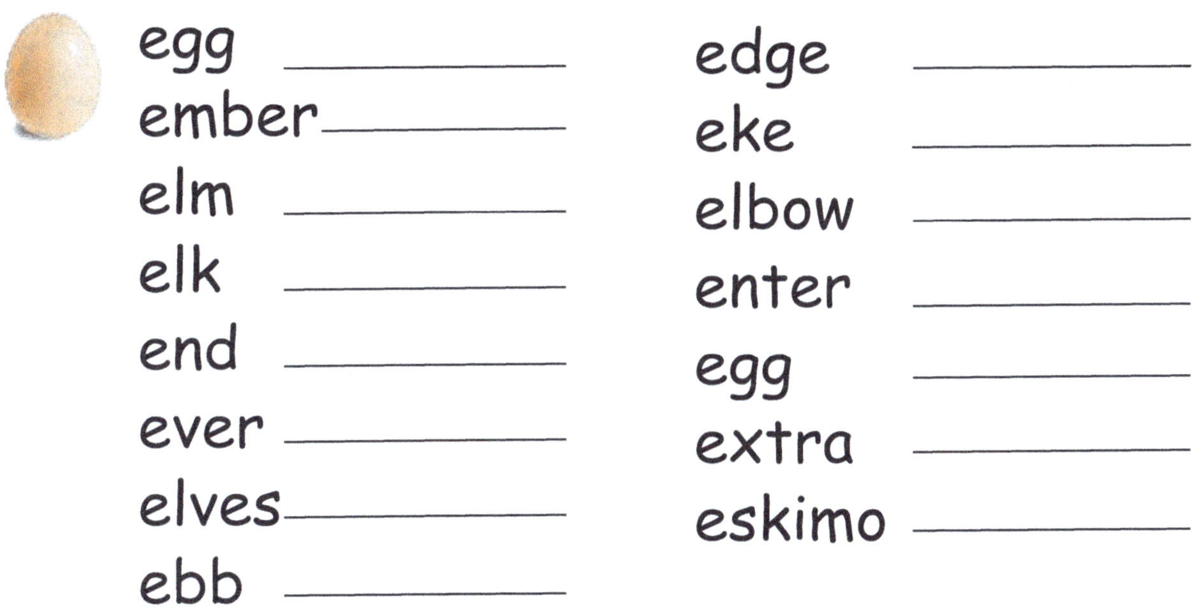

egg __________	edge __________
ember __________	eke __________
elm __________	elbow __________
elk __________	enter __________
end __________	egg __________
ever __________	extra __________
elves __________	eskimo __________
ebb __________	

d. Fill in the missing 'e' sound:

_njoy   f_n   d_ntist   sl_nder
_nemy   m_mber   f_ll   wh_n
_gg   tr_mble

e. Read these words and check out their
    meanings in your dictionary.

envelope	elephant	wet	hen
step	bell	elbow	desk
pet	pencil		

f. Make a sentence with each word

envelope : <u>The pen is in the envelope</u>

elephant ___________________________

wet _______________________________

hen _______________________________

step ______________________________

bell ______________________________

elbow _____________________________

desk ______________________________

pet _______________________________

pencil ____________________________

Draw a pencil

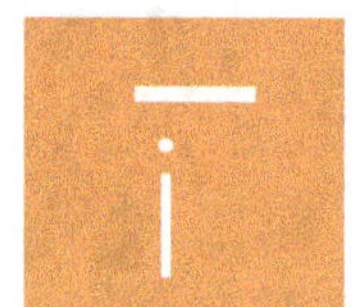

/I/

a. Say these words out, then write them on the
   lines provided.

dig _______________	bill _______________
fib _______________	pimple _______________
gin _______________	ring _______________
him _______________	simple _______________
lima _______________	vin _______________
bib _______________	nip _______________

b. Underline the 'i' sound

fin	gig	wiggle	zip	ship
twig	shingle	whiz	quit	
indigo	visit	film		

c. Some words have the 'i' sound at the beginning.
   Say the words out and write them on the lines
   provided:

Ink _______________	ilk _______________
imp _______________	india _______________

ink ________________   inject ________________

igloo ________________   inn ________________

idiot ________________   insect ________________

iguana ________________   internet ________________

imam ________________   into ________________

indigo ________________

d. Fill in the missing i sound

h_s	_ll	wh_z	_mportant
s_xty	qu_z	_gloo	_nsect
sh_p	_nternet		

e. Read these words and check out their meanings in your dictionary:

Twin	iguana	pig	igloo
ship	bin	india	important
lid	insect		

f. Make a sentence with each word:

twin _______________________________

____

ship _______________________________

lid _______________________________

iguana _______________________________

bin _______________________________

insect _______________________________

pig _______________________________

India _______________________________

igloo _______________________________

important _______________________________

g. Daw a ship

a. Write five words for each sound:

a	e	i
______	______	______
______	______	______
______	______	______
______	______	______
______	______	______

b. Learn how to spell the following words:

Classroom   axle   keg   pepper
simple   milk   film   insect
import   elephant   pizza   basket
elm   extra   pasta   whiz

c. Use these words to complete the following

____ra   c____m   p____a

p__r   k____g   i____ct   b____t

i__________nt   w__z

Note:
Select any 10 words to use as dictation exercise with your learners. Copy out all the words on your chalk board first.

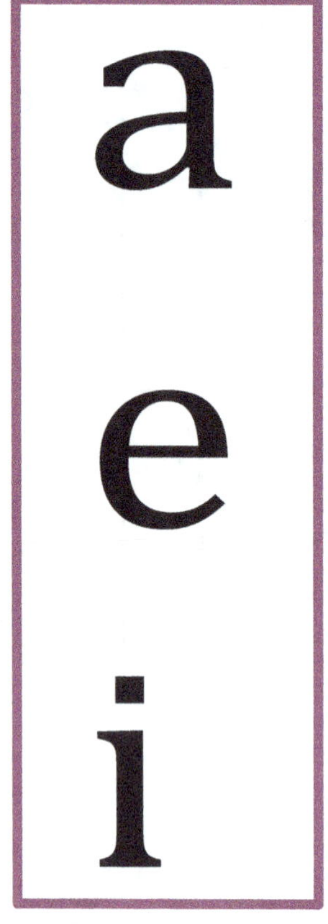

d. complete the following sentences.
   The diagram above will help you.

1. The ______ is on the __________

2. Ali placed the ______ in the ______

3. The ________ hit the __________

4. An ________ is in the ________

5. I have an ______ and a __________

e. Read the rhyme (Like Farmer in the Dell):

There are ants on the axe 2x
a,a,a,a,a,a, there are ants on the axe.
There are eggs in the pen 2x
e,e,e,e,e,e, there are eggs in the pen.
There is ink in the inn 2x
i,i,i,i,i,i, there is ink in the inn

f. <u>Draw an insect</u>

/ɒ/, /ɔ/, /ə/

a. Say these words out then write them in the lines provided

bob _______   otter _______   shop _______

clot _______   jota _______   towel _______

dot _______   lobster _______   volume _______

got _______   stop _______   donkey _______

b. Underline the 'o' sound:

not   pot   robin   smog

bottle   cod   frog   gossip

hog   job   log   month

ton   cock   wobble   flock

c. Say these words out and write them on the lines provided:

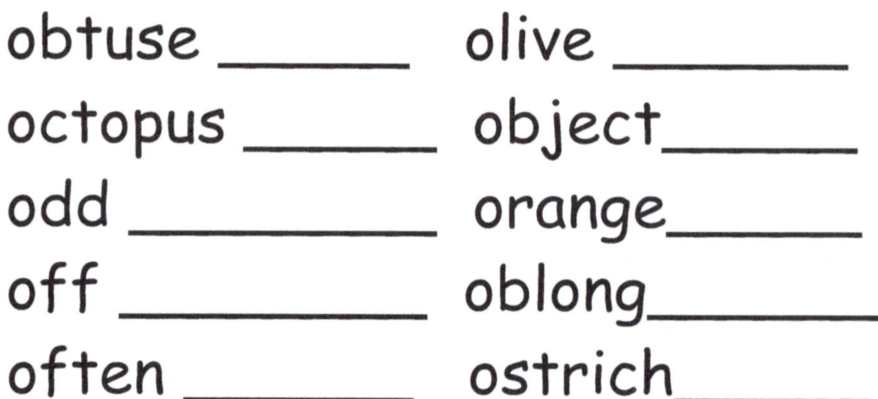

obtuse _______   olive _______

octopus _______   object _______

odd _______   orange _______

off _______   oblong _______

often _______   ostrich _______

otter——————— odd ——————

oscar——————— office ————

d. From the box select all the words with 'ŏ'
   sound and write them on the lines provided.

Flop   ask   jog   octopus
big   cod   floss   apple
   toddler   bottle
            olive   pebble
orange   absence   ink   cop

———————   ———————   ———————   ———————

———————   ———————   ———————   ———————

———————   ———————

e. Find out the meanings of these words from
   your dictionary:

frog   ostrich   omit   lobster
job   rob   omellette   nod
fox   monkey   possible

f. Make a sentence with each word:

1. Possible: <u>It is possible to get it done. Do it.</u>

2. Lobster

3. Rob

4. Nod

5. Monkey

6. Ostrich

7. Fox

8. Job

9. Frog

10. Omellette

<u>Draw a frog</u>

 /ʌ/

a. Say these words out, then write them on the lines provided:

Bug___________   funny___________

cup___________   gutter___________

cutlass___________   hum___________

dug___________   hungry___________

duster___________   jump___________

flub___________   just___________

b. Fill in the 'u' sound and say the word

b _ s   n _ mber   br _ sh

p _ p   n _ ts   s _ m

l _ ng   pl _ m   sh _ t

m _ ch   p _ ppy   t _ g

dr _ m   r _ t   t _ ck

Note: The 'u' sound here sounds /ˆ / or º
The sound /ju/ or 'you' would come later

c. Say these words out and write them on the
    lines provided:

under _______________   until _______________

up _______________   unless _______________

upon _______________   urgent _______________

us _______________   ugly _______________

urn _______________   uplift _______________

umbrella _______________   upper _______________

uncle _______________   undies _______________

undo _______________

d. Write five words each for 'u'

starting a word	in the middle of a word
_______________	_______________
_______________	_______________
_______________	_______________
_______________	_______________
_______________	_______________

e. Use your dictionary to find out the meaning
   of these words:

bug   gum   jump   lung   duster
cup   umbrella   under   cutlass
brush   uncle   up   bucket
urn   nurse

f. Make a sentence with each of these words:

1. Bug _______________________________________

2. Lung _______________________________________

3. Duster _______________________________________

4. Uncle _______________________________________

5. Umbrella _______________________________________

6. Nurse _______________________________________

7. Cup _______________________________________

8. Bucket _______________________________________

9. Jump _______________________________________

10. Under _______________________________________

g. Draw a bug

O, U

a. Write five words for each sound

O	U
__________	__________
__________	__________
__________	__________
__________	__________
__________	__________

b. Learn how to spell these words

orange	bottle	hungry	umbrella
lung	upon	monk	ostrich
towel	odd	just	undies
us	nurse	fox	olive
topic	gum	ugly	rotten

Use the words in the box to complete the following

1. _ p _ n
2. _ _ _ k
3. n _ _ se
4. r _ _ _ _ _ n
5. _ _ st

6. f _ _
7. b _ _ tle
8. _ str _ _ _
9. t _ _ _ l
10. _ r _ _ g _

C.

Complete the following sentences. The diagram above will help you.

1. The _______ is _______ the table
2. I cut the _______ with a _______
3. The _______ has an _______
4. The _______ is in the _______
5. The _______ ate the _______

Circle the sound in the words provided:

a. a ___ @ngle   battle   plasma   wrap

   e ___ spell   evict   end   plenty

   I ___ indigo   Pitt   sit   mix

   o ___ object   mop   brother box.

   u ___ drum   spun   up   under

b. Write five words for each sound:

a	e	i	o	u	

c. Make a sentence with each word:

fell ________________________________

Skip ________________________________

gas _________________________________

map _________________________________

plum ________________________________

Fact Find 1

A van is a big car. It is not as big as a truck. It has windows at the sides. Or, it may have no windows in its back half. It can carry people, bags, cases or mail.

Draw a van

a. Say these words out then write them
   on the lines provided:

bade ——————————   vane ——————————

cape ——————————   cake ——————————

fate ——————————   bake ——————————

gate ——————————   tape ——————————

hate ——————————   fade ——————————

Read, then underline the long 'a' sound

1. Bake me a cake, please.

2. I will pay for it.

3. He hates to stay away.

4. He is by the gate.

5. I can play a tape.

Note:
This set of long vowels produce the same sound as
their capital letters when they appear singly.
Long a =A=/ei/(oral English sound) . Long e=E=/i:/.
Long i=I=/ai/|. o=/ow/ u |yu|

6. The rats ate the poison.

____

7. Kate sings with a thin voice.

____

8. Point at the man.

____

9. The kettle is boiling.

____

10. He gave the beggar a coin.

____

PETER AND THE BIRD

One day, a farmer named Peter went to his farm.
He found that his trap had caught a bird. He was very happy because he felt he had got a meal for his family. He held the bird in his hand and thought of what his wife would do with it. He imagined eating Pounded yam with Egusi soup made from bird meat.
The bird looked at Peter and said, "Shame, Is this all you could catch- a bony bird like me? I am only feathers. My meat can't even fill your little boy's tummy. Besides, my meat is bitter. Just let me go. Catch a squirrel instead and take it to your wife, she will be happy you did".

Peter looked at the bird and thought
the bird was right: it had no weight and
it would be a waste of his time preserving
it to take home.
         So he let the bird go.
No sooner was the bird free, than it flew
and perched on a tree close to Peter.

 Then it started singing:
Peter has lost some fleshy meat
He has lost some fleshy meat ,2x
Ha,ha,ha,ha

On hearing this, Peter tried to catch
the bird again but the bird flew away.

Peter became very sad because he had
foolishly allowed the bird to go .
He went home without any food for
his family .
Lesson: A bird in hand is worth ten in the
          bush.

Look at the picture. What do you see?

ch, ph, sh, th, wh, ng

ch   /tʃ/ tch

a. Say each word out and write them out

bea**ch** ___________	ma**tch** ___________
tea**ch**er__________	re**tch**___________
chairman ________	sti**tch**__________
charm __________	pa**tch** __________
chunk __________	wi**tch** __________
par**ch**ed _________	wa**tch**__________
mar**ch** __________	di**tch** __________
pin**ch** __________	ma**tch** __________
ri**ch** ___________	ba**tch**__________
chur**ch** ________	fe**tch** __________

Note: These are consonant digraphs - A combination of two consonant letters that represent one sound.
To pronounce ch: The teeth are held together with the lips pointing out - tch
Careful: Some children tend to subtitute sh for this

b. Add 'ch' to these letters and read the words out:

star_ _	wat _ _	win _ _
ya _ _ t	in _ _	whi _ _
su _ _	mu _ _	lea _ _
_ _ arm	cat _ _	_ _ eck
_ _ icken	_ _ ief	ea _ _

c. Make a sentence with each word:

rich: Amir's father is rich.

starch: ____________________

bench: ____________________

chair: ____________________

chicken ____________________

batch _______________________

____

retch _______________________

____

fetch _______________________

____

catch _______________________

____

match _______________________

____

d. Draw and colour a chair

____

ph /f/

a. Say each word, then write the words out:

camphor	graph
caliph	hyphen
dolphin	lymph
geography	nymph
orphan	oomph
phase	phantom
pharmacy	phone
photo	physics

b. Add 'ph' to these letters and then read the words formed:

1. em _ _ asis
2. tro _ _ y
3. syl _ _

4. cali _ _
5. _ _ ysical
6. lym _ _

Note:ph - these two letters make a 'f' sound

7. or _ _ an   9. _ _ ase
8. oom _ _   10. ty_ _ oon

c. Make a sentence with each word:

1. dolphin ______________________________

____

2. photo ______________________________

____

3. phone ______________________________

____

4. phase ______________________________

____

5. pharmacy ______________________________

____

6. graph ______________________________

____

7. trophy

8. orphan

9. typhoid

10. geography

d. Draw and colour a phone

sh /ʃ/

a. Say each word out, then write the words on the
   lines provided:

ash ___________	dish ___________
bash ___________	cash ___________
brush ___________	ship ___________
blush ___________	wish ___________
cash ___________	wash ___________
crash ___________	shoe ___________
cashew ___________	shop ___________
flash ___________	show ___________
fish ___________	shout ___________
marsh mallow ___________	

b.

> ash ship show cashew
> shout cash marshmallow
> harsh
> dish brush crash

Find the correct word from the box above that these sentences describe:

1. What you use to pay for something ____________

2. A boat that sails on sea ____________

3. A soft sweet made from sugar and egg that feels elastic when you chew it ____________

4. A shallow bowl for food ____________

5. What you use to smoothen your hair ____________

6. He is very strict ____________

7. What is left after fire has died out ____________

8. A fruit that grows on tree _______________________

9. It fell with a loud sound _______________________

10. He spoke out loudly _______________________

c. Add 'sh' to these letters and read the words out:

_ _ eep   fi _ _   _ _ irt

blu _ _   wi _ _   tra _ _

me _ _   _ _ allow   _ _ oot

fle _ _

d. Make a sentence with each word:

1. shoe   _______________________

____

2. sharp   _______________________

____

3. warsh   _______________________

____

4. sheep   ___________________________

  ____

5. fish   ___________________________

  ____

6. she   ___________________________

  ____

7. show   ___________________________

  ____

8. shop   ___________________________

  ____

9. wish   ___________________________

  ____

10. trash   ___________________________

  ____

th /θ/,   **th** /ð/

a. Say each word and write them out

ba**th** __________	**th**e __________
dea**th** __________	**th**is __________
ear**th** __________	**th**ere __________
fif**th** __________	soo**th**e __________
gir**th** __________	li**th**e __________
heal**th** __________	wi**th** __________
sou**th** __________	**th**at __________
too**th** __________	**th**eir __________
oa**th** __________	**th**em __________
think __________	**th**an __________
thaw __________	**th**ese __________

Note: There are two sounds treated here. They are produced whenthe tip of the tongue touches the upper incisors. The tongue should protrude sllghtly, more for /θ/ than / /,

b. Add 'th' to these letters and read the words out:

boo_ _   mo _ _   nor _ _
clo _ _   mo _ _ er   soo _ _ e
four _ _   fa _ _ er   ra _ _ er
_ _ ey   _ _ ree   _ _ irst

c. Circle the words that have 'th' sound

chicken   thrust   tomato   such
fish   most   feet   mother
cloth   show   sheep   hate
flat   man   tooth   start
cheat   smooth float   dirt

d. Make a sentence with each word:

1. tooth   _______________________________

____

2. cloth   _______________________________

____

3. mother

4. with

5. these

6. fourth

7. brother

8. path

9. that

10. something

a. Read these. Note the difference in sound. Then write each word out:

who _______________	while _______________
whole _______________	whiz _______________
whom _______________	whistle _______________
whose _______________	wheel _______________
whoever _______________	wheel barrow _______________
wholly _______________	white _______________
wholesome _______________	whisker _______________
wholesale _______________	whoop_______________

b. Add 'wh' to these letters and read the words out:

_ _ oop	_ _ ose	_ _ isk
_ _ y	_ _ eeze	_ _ isper
_ _ ich	_ _ ile	_ _ ite
_ _ o	_ _ ip	_ _ ether

c. Circle the word that has 'wh':

1. waist   wrist   watch   whisper
2. women   where   work   world
3. wonder   wheel   well   water
4. whom   window   willow   worse
5. write   went   whisk   warm

d. Write out their names. Use words from the box:

_________   _________   _________

_________   _________

white
wheel
whistle
whisker
whale

e. Make a sentence with each word

1. white _______________________

____

2. wheel barrow _______________________

____

3. who _______________________

____

4. which _______________________

____

5. whip _______________________

____

6. why _______________________

____

7. whale _______________________

____

8. where _______________________

____

9. what _______________________

____

10. whether _______________________

____

ng /ŋ/

a. Say each word out. Then write them

song ________________   single ______________

long ________________   thing______________

strong ______________   among ____________

throng ______________   belong ____________

hongkong ____________   fling ____________

bing ________________   cling ____________

sing ________________   mingle____________

b. Add 'ng' to these letters and read the words out:

spri _ _   wi _ _   ka _ _ aroo

sti _ _   ba _ _ le   E _ _ lish

ba _ _   ma _ _ le   ha _ _

si _ _ le

c. Make a sentence with each word:

1. sing _______________________________

____

2. kangaroo _______________________________

____

3. long _______________________________

____

4. finger _______________________________

____

5. tingle _______________________________

____

6. English _______________________________

____

7. sting _______________________________

____

8. bangle _______________________________

____

9. hang _______________________________

____

10. spring _______________________________

____

a. Write five words for each of these sounds:

ch	ph	sh	th
___	___	___	___
___	___	___	___
___	___	___	___
___	___	___	___
___	___	___	___

wh	ng
___	___
___	___
___	___
___	___
___	___

b. Circle the correct word for each sound indicated:

ch	foot (c)hoose shame boot shop style rich tooth
ph	paint pepper packet photo faint fall phone pester
sh	sheep sister silly star check polish match bench
th	temper test that tart wimp with fat tilt
wh	wire wheel water waist washer wife white wrist
ng	chant bangle pitch song English ranch shirt shark

c. Fill in the correct words:

> pharmacy   health   orphan
> nothing   show   whisper   pitch
> punch   chairman   ring

1. It is _________ black.
2. Rali spoke in a ___________.
3. There is _______ wrong with him.
4. ________ me your book please.
5. The _________ child is hungry.
6. She gave the bag a ___________.
7. Mr. Bello is the _________ of this occasion.
8. She will get the drug from the ___________.
9. The bell is going to _____________.
10. My grandmother is in good _____________.

d. Read these sentences

1. She chose the ship over the yacht.
2. The beef broth is sharp.
3. The sun shall soon shine.
4. Who will blow the whistle?
5. The champion raised the trophy high.
6. She chomped on the nuts with her bad tooth.
7. My mother added a pinch of salt to the fish.
8. He went through the Math test in a flash.
9. Their shop is fifth on the street.
10. How long did you stay in Hong kong?

e. Draw a fish in a dish.

An Eclipse

Look at the diagram above. Talk about it in class with your teacher.

Read this passage

An eclipse

Sometimes, the moon-in its path around the Earth- passes between the sun and the Earth. It thus, blots out the sun's rays and the day grows dark in some parts of the world. This is called a Solar Eclipse.

Big and Bold

An ostrich is not an ordinary bird. It is the largest and heaviest living bird. It has beautiful long feathers, but it cannot fly because of its size.

An ostrich is built for running. It can take giant steps. It can sprint like a runner too. Even the birds wings help it to run.

If an ostrich needs to dash away, if spreads its wings. The wings keep the ostrich balanced. The wings also help an ostrich to make sharp turns to confuse its enemy. It is a remarkable bird.

Cereal

Rice, corn and wheat are called cereal grasses because they are grown mostly as food. Rice, corn and wheat are grown in different ways, but their grains or seed are a rich source of food.

Rice grows in field called paddies that are flooded with water. Rice is the most important food for many people in the word. Its stems called 'straw' are used to make rugs and roots.

Corn is planted in rows in large field. Farmers pump water between the rows. One stalk of corn can grow up to 15feet high. It holds between one and four ears of corn. The seeds or kernels on each ear are made into corn flakes, pop corn and corn chips They can also be eaten as corn nubbin. Corn is also used to make fuel, crayons and dyes.

Wheat is one of the first grasses grown by people. Its does not need a lot of water to grow. Wheat is used to make spaghetti and cereal. Wheat flour is used in baked goods. The straw makes a good bedding for animals.

Some words helps us to read better. They are called articles. Articles show how definite a noun is.
The articles are:

a   an   the

Read these sentences:

a

1. He is a boy.
2. She has a big doll.
3. My brother is a doctor.
4. We are in a car.
5. My teacher is a woman.

an

1. The hen has an egg.
2. Please give him an umbrella.
3. I can eat an orange.
4. Give the horse an apple.
5. Musa has an ink pot.

Note: 'the' is used for known (definite) singular or plural nouns. 'a' and 'an'- for singular indefinite nouns. 'a' is used before consonant sounds. 'an' is used for vowel sounds.

6. I have **an** hour of work.

7. She has **an** x-ray.

8. It was **an** honor working with you.

<u>the</u>

1. Show me **the** ball.
2. Give her **the** pencils.
3. He is in **the** class.
4. Go to **the** market.
5. Take **the** dress.
6. She is in **the** university.

Quantifiers: Use of some, any, much and many,

<u>much and many</u>
<u>much</u>

1. The water in the tank is **much**.

2. There is not **much** fuel left in the tank.

3. Do we have **much** time?

Note: the use of these quantifiers depends on if the noun is countable or uncountable

4. He ate too much rice.
5. We do not need much water.

<u>many</u>
1. He has many pencils.
2. There are many people in this room.
3. We were many taking a walk.
4. How many pots are there?
5. How many hands are up?

<u>Some and any</u>

Some - A small quantity
1. Give me some water.
2. I have some friends in the senior class.
3. My mother gave me some bread.
4. Add some sugar and milk to your tea.
5. Would you like some more tea?

<u>any (small or all)</u>

1. Do you have any shoes?
2. He does not have any clothes.
3. I don't have any friends.
4. He is open to any suggestions.
5. Do you have any ice cream left?

THE DOG AND HIS BONE

A dog was waiting outside a butcher's
shop one day, as he often did, looking as
hungry and sad as he could.
That day, the butcher saw him, took
pity on him and threw him a bone.
 The dog trotted away,happy as could be, his
tail wagging as he went, thinking of where
he would bury the bone and how good it
would taste after a week or two.

Before getting to his home, he had to
cross a little footbridge over a stream.
 He was padding across when something
caught his eye, he saw another dog, just below
 him, staring at him from the still waters.

What a big bone this dog has! he thought, looking enviously at it. It's much bigger than mine. I want it too! Aargh!!!. With that, he tried to snatch it from the other dog.

As he opened his mouth to do that, his precious bone slipped out and fell into the deep still waters. He tried to get it back but the water was too deep. The bone was gone for good.

Only then, did he realize the mistake he had made, how silly he had been. There had been no other dog, no other bone, only his own reflection in the water. He had been too greedy to notice or to think before acting.

He clambered out of the river, shook himself dry and walked off home, his tail between his legs, feeling very stupid and very cross with himself.

Moral Lesson:

ENOUGH IS AS GOOD AS A FEAST.
DON'T BE GREEDY

THE WOLF AND THE SHEPHERD'S SON

Once upon a time, a shepherd thought his son was old enough now to guard sheep all by himself. So he sent him off with the flock into the hills one morning. "What if a wolf comes along?" the boy asked.

"Just give us a shout," his father replied, "and we'll come and frighten him off."

Day after day the shepherd's son watched over his father's sheep peacefully. The days were hot and long. Nothing new ever seemed to happen. After a while, he began to feel very bored.

So he thought he'd make something happen - just for fun.

Leaving his sheep grazing peacefully, he ran over the hill, waving his arms and shouting as loud as he could, "Wolf! Wolf!"

Just as he had hoped, all the villagers, his father amongst them, stopped everything they were doing. and came running with their sticks to drive away the wolf.

But of course, as they soon discovered, there was no wolf.

"Fooled you! Fooled you!" laughed the shepherd's son. But neither his father nor the villagers thought it was funny at all.

They returned to the village in anger.
 Some days later, the shepherd's son played the same trick again.

"Wolf! Wolf!" he cried at the top of his voice, and again all the villagers came running. "Fooled you! Fooled you!" he laughed again. But no one else was laughing and his father was very angry indeed.

Then, the very next day, as the shepherd's son sat watching his sheep, he really did see a wolf slinking towards the sheep through the long grass. He leapt to his feet at once and ran over the hill, shouting as loud as he could, "Wolf! Wolf!"

But neither his father nor villagers came. He ran all the way down , screaming at the top of his voice, but it seemed no one had heard him because none of them believed him, not this time.

"He tricked us once, he tricked us twice," his father said. "He 'll not trick us a third time. There is no wolf. He's just playing games."

"There really is a wolf, he cried." But no one would listen to him.

Meanwhile the wolf attacked the flock and killed all the sheep it could. This left him very sad and full of regrets. He swore never to raise a false alarm again,

Moral lesson:

NO ONE BELIEVES A LIAR
EVEN WHEN HE IS TELLING THE TRUTH.

These are some of the words we come across in all reading. Take note of them:

a	from	one	know
about	had	said	we
all	have	she	were
an	he	that	what
are	how	their	when
as	I	them	which
at	if	then	will
be	is	there	with
but	in	they	you
by	it	this	your
can	many	to	just
do	of	too	little
each	not	two	again
for	on	up	other
an	was	out	would

Happy Children

ALL ABOUT ME

My Name is ________________________

I am ________________________ years old

I am in ________________________

The name of my school is ________________________

____

My friend's name is ________________________

I like eating ________________________

Everyday I ________________________

Draw yourself here

This is me

A |ei|	B |bi|	C |si|	D |di|
E |i|	F |ef|	G |gi|	H |eich|
I |ai|	J |yei|	K |key|	L |el|
M |em|	N |en|	O |ou|	P |pi|
Q |kiu|	R |ar|	S |es|	T |ti|
U |yu|	V |vi|	W |double yu|	
X |eks|	Y |uai|	Z |zed|	

NOTE